Conversations
on

Let's Pretend This Never Happened
Jenny Lawson

By dailyBooks

Tips for Using dailyBooks Conversation Starters:

EVERY GOOD BOOK CONTAINS A WORLD FAR DEEPER THAN the surface of its pages. The characters and their world come alive through the words on the pages, yet the characters and its world still live on. Questions herein are designed to bring us beneath the surface of the page and invite us into the world that lives on. These questions can be used to:

- Foster a deeper understanding of the book
- Promote an atmosphere of discussion for groups
- Assist in the study of the book, either individually or corporately
- Explore unseen realms of the book as never seen before

About Us:

THROUGH YEARS OF EXPERIENCE AND FIELD EXPERTISE, from newspaper featured book clubs to local library chapters, *dailyBooks* can bring your book discussion to life. Host your book party as we discuss some of today's most widely read books.

Table of Contents

Introducing *Let's Pretend This Never Happened*

IN *LET'S PRETEND THIS NEVER HAPPENED*, American author Jenny Lawson recounts some of the most critical moments in her life, from her childhood in rural Texas to her high school years and married life.

Growing up, Lawson wanted nothing more than to fit in. That didn't prove to be easy given her unconventional childhood. The daughter of a taxidermist, she lived in poverty in a little town, where her swimming pool was a cistern for washing hogs. In high school, she was the goth girl who just didn't quite fit in.

Lawson then takes readers through her own family life—marrying Victor, a man who is her polar opposite, at 22 and taking a job in human resources. She shares anecdotes from her 15-year marriage, including her series of miscarriages before giving birth to her daughter, Hailey.

Lawson also shares her writing journey, from starting her blog, *The Bloggess*, in 2007 (mainly to have a platform to write using foul language) to attempting to make female friends at a bloggers' retreat in California.

Lawson's bizarre life and her unique writing provided her with an effective coping mechanism. She discovered humor in even the most traumatic places and events and produced this laugh-out-loud piece of work.

Let's Pretend This Never Happened, although outrageously funny, is not for the faint of heart. Lawson, with her signature dark humor and crude writing, touches on some serious matters such as anxiety disorders, anorexia, suicidal thoughts, and miscarriages.

The book is hilarious yet poignant. In it, Lawson realizes, with the help of her ever-supportive husband and daughter, that the moments we want to leave behind are the very ones that bring us to where we are today.

The *New Yorks Times* bestseller *Let's Pretend This Never Happened* is Lawson's literary debut and was released on April 17, 2012. Her follow-up book titled *Furiously Happy* was released on September 22, 2015, and reached number one on the *New York Times* bestseller. She resides in the Texas Hill Country with her husband and daughter.

Introducing the Author

MOST KNOWN FOR HER IRREVERENT WRITING STYLE, impeccable humor, and unforgiving wit, American journalist, blogger, and author Jenny Lawson, also known as The Bloggess (thebloggess.com), makes readers laugh out loud and sometimes even question their sanity. The immensely gifted writer takes the craziest thoughts from her readers' heads—those they'd rather not say out loud—and dares to put them on paper.

Lawson is the author of the *New York Times* bestselling memoir *Let's Pretend This Never Happened*, her literary debut, which was released on April 17, 2012. Her follow-up book titled *Furiously Happy* was released on September of 2015 and reached number one on the *New York Times* bestseller list on July of 2016. Lawson, who reportedly suffers from ADD and anxiety disorder, is a graduate of Angelo State University. She lives in the Texas Hill Country with her husband and daughter.

Aside from being the author of *The Bloggess*, Lawson formerly co-authored the *Houston Chronicle*'s *Good Mom/Bad Mom* and was a columnist for *SexIs* magazine and recognized by Nielsen ratings as a Top 50 Most Powerful Mom Bloggers, and her website thebloggess.com was listed by *Forbes* as one of the Top 100 Websites for Women.

Lawson was also a finalist for Best Writing and Most Humorous Writer, and in 2011, additionally for the Weblog of the Year. She was called the "Greatest Person of the Day" in 2011 by *The Huffington Post* for her fundraising efforts for struggling families the year before.

Not for the faint of heart, Lawson's no-nonsense, crass, and dark humor continues to gain her a strong following both online and in print. Part hysterical, part bizarre, and part vulgar, Lawson's writings are nothing short of difficult to put down.

Discussion Questions

. . . .

question 1

The book's subtitle reads, A Mostly True Memoir, which the author explains in the opening page. Do you think the storytelling being "mostly true"—as opposed to being "entirely true"—was effective? Why or why not?

. . . .

question 2

In the book, the author retells her childhood growing up in the small town in Texas. Which of her childhood experiences do you share or to which ones can you relate?

question 3

The author describes her hometown as "violently rural." How do
you think this environment shaped her personality growing up?

. . . .

question 4

    The book touches on both themes of family life and individuality. Which theme stood out to you more and why?

. . . .

question 5

The book also tackles serious topics including suicidal tendencies, anorexia, mental illness, and miscarriages, but it is still considered a humor piece. What do you think made the two contrasting elements - seriousness and humor - work together in the book?

. . . .

question 6

Did any of the author's sensitive anecdotes make you feel
uncomfortable? If so, which one was it, and why do you think
you responded that way?

. . . .

· ·

question 7

The author also talked about her parents' unconventional ways of raising her. How do you think her upbringing affected her adulthood?

· ·

. . . .

question 8

The author and her husband Victor are very different from each other, especially in terms of their principles, personalities, and political backgrounds. What do you think has made their marriage work despite their differences?

. . . .

. . . .

question 9

The author's husband tried to set up a special proposal for her,
which didn't go according to plan. Did you ever find yourself in a
situation where your special plans went awry? How did you deal
with it?

. . . .

. . . .

question 10

In the book, Lawson also discusses her realization that home, for her, is wherever her husband Victor is. What is your concept of home?

. . . .

· ·

question 11

The author also talks about her mental health issues in the book.
How did her revelation affect your perception of her life story?
Were you able to understand her more or less?

· ·

. . . .

question 12

In the book, the author uses footnotes, disclaimers, and strikethroughs while telling her life story. What effect did these elements have on you as a reader? Did you find these limiting or interrupting?

. . . .

question 13

The book was reportedly reviewed by Lawson's family members before it was published. Do you think this was necessary? How do you think it affected the creative process of the author? Why do you think she chose to let her family members review the book first?

question 14

Out of all the family members and other individuals mentioned in the book, which one resonated most with you? How so?

–

. . . .

question 15

Throughout the book, the author retells rather mortifying
moments in her life that a person would normally want to
pretend never happened. Which moments in your life make you
feel this way?

. . . .

question 16

The book was mostly well-received upon release, became a *New York Times* bestseller, and also won Goodread's Best Humor Book of 2012. Do you think the book deserves the success it now enjoys? Why or why not?

. . . .

question 17

Some reviews find the author's storytelling faulty and "all over
the place." Do you agree? Why or why not?

. . . .

question 18

Readers with a dark sense of humor can most appreciate the book. How do you think a different type of reader, say a more sensitive one, could go about reading the book?

question 19

Lawson is known for her dark sense of humor and sharpness in writing. Did her storytelling make you laugh out loud? Was it effective in rousing your emotions, and if so, how?

· ·

. . . .

question 20

How do you think the book would have been received had the author's story been used to inspire and create a work of fiction instead? Would it make any difference at all?

. . . .

question 21

Would you agree that the book is the type of read that's difficult
to put down? Why or why not?

. . . .

question 22

The author revealed that it took her 11 years to finish the book.
While reading the book, did it feel like it was worked on for that
long?

. . . .

. . . .

question 23

Other reviews mention how certain revelations of the author can make the reader cringe. Did you experience this while reading the book? Where in the book do you think the author may have taken it too far?

. . . .

. . . .

question 24

Due to the outrageous and unbelievable stories in Lawson's book, it's unavoidable to have accusations of her embellishing her stories. How do you think she tried to address this in the book?

. . . .

. . . .

question 25

Even before the publication of the book, Lawson already had a
following online as a blogger. Do you think this helped the book
to be a success? Why or why not?

. . . .

. . . .

question 26

Lawson is also famous for her blog titled *The Bloggess*. Have you read the author's writings before reading the book? What was your impression of her?

. . . .

. . . .

question 27

In her blog, the author said she worked on the book for 11 years. Why do you think it took so long? Would you engage in a project that took that long?

. . . .

. . . .

question 28

Lawson's writing has been called foul, inappropriate, and vulgar.
How do you feel about her writing style?

. . . .

· ·

question 29

Lawson is known to be suffering from ADD and anxiety disorder.
Knowing this about the author, how do you think her condition
affects her storytelling?

· ·

question 30

Lawson is often compared to fellow author David Sedaris. Do you agree? What do you think are their similarities and/or differences?

. . . .

question 31

In the book, the author reveals her own embarrassing life stories to deliver a narrative. If you were to write your own memoir, would you also be open to sharing the really outrageous anecdotes in your life?

. . . .

. . . .

question 32

The Internet helped the author connect with like-minded people and make friends before going on a blogger's retreat. Would you have done the same if you were trying to make new friends?

. . . .

. . . .

question 33

After an incident in school involving a turkey, Lawson decided to stop trying to fit in. What do you think would have happened if she didn't make that decision then?

. . . .

. . . .

question 34

The author and her husband are polar opposites. Would you choose to marry someone who is very different from you in terms of background and personality?

. . . .

. . . .

question 35

The author had a very eccentric childhood and unconventional upbringing. What do you think would have changed in her life had she had a more "normal" childhood?

. . . .

question 36

The book is written in a very in-your-face tone. How do you think the book would have turned out if the tone was more melancholic and serious? Would you have enjoyed it as much?

. . . .

question 37

If you were to live the eccentric childhood the author had, would you also react to the same experiences the same way? If not, what would be the difference in your way of handling the situation?

. . . .

. . . .

question 38

The author laughs at some really traumatizing life events, like
suffering from anorexia and miscarriages. Looking back at your
own trying moments, would you also react to them with humor?

. . . .

Quiz Questions

. . . .

question 39

Lawson's father was a _____, caused their family to
have animals like raccoons, turkeys, and bobcats at home

. . . .

. . . .

question 40

_____was the name of the leader of the group of
turkeys Lawson's father once brought home

. . . .

question 41

True or false: Lawson and her husband both attended Harvard University.

. . . .

question 42

True or false: Lawson described her hometown as "Violently rural."

. . . .

question 43

Lawson used _____ to connect with possible
female friends before attending a bloggers' retreat?

. . . .

question 44

Lawson's career was in _____ before
becoming a writer.

. . . .

. . . .

question 45

True or False: The author lived in poverty during her younger years.

. . . .

question 46

Lawson was born and raised in _____.

. . . .

question 47

Lawson suffers from _____.

. . . .

question 48

True or false: The author spent 6 months writing this book.

question 49

The author uses _____ to make light of the
heavy anecdotes in her book.

question 50

The two major themes tackled in the book are
_____ and _____.

Quiz Answers

1. Taxidermist
2. Jenkins
3. False; Angelo State University
4. True
5. Internet
6. HR
7. True
8. Wall, Texas
9. Anxiety disorder
10. False; 11
11. humor
12. family / individuality

THE END

Want to promote your book group? Register here.

Made in the USA
Monee, IL
02 August 2024

63125558R00039